ECHOES OF FAITH

With thanks to friends and family and everyone who has encouraged me to write.

"the lord is my light and my salvation-whom shall I fear?"
Psalm 27

This is my fourth book following the trilogy **Let's make tea out of roses**

Roses in the tea caddy and **Tea and afternoon roses.**

The subjects are of *Spirit* and *Nature* and touching on *conflict in the present world and climate*, with warm tones of hope and optimism.

From *"only to draw the petal from her sling as she keeps on glimpsing the Spring"* to *"ceaseless is the blue blown glass the circle of the dreaded stars."*

Enjoy the Read,

Claire.

Cover design by the author

Instagram:@everywordisamemory

Editor: Sharon Andrews, Instagram:@inksomnia_poetry

With love and thanks to Sharon.

Contents

A cluster of grape rock 5

Berry 6

Blown away world 7

Ceaseless is the blue blown glass 8

Chastise me with your whip 9

Do not let the geese 10

Don't look into 11

Gowns of youthful sounds 12

I sleep in rows of *big flowers* 13

Keepsakes 14

Like sycamore seeds 15

Morning 16

New lilac 18

No nature is clinging 19

Request 20

Seasonal tides 21

The angels of the earth 22

The blue and yellow war 23

The ebb 24

The hyacinth 25

The night flower 26

The petal 27
The sun quickens 28
The temptress 29
The waves cartwheel 30
Through the archway 31
un coup d'oeil 32
What dens of peacefulness 33

A cluster of grape rock

Damson grey,
Sits along the quickening
Wool of earth.

Below the rubble
Velvet moles
Hustle in gowns
Of yellow,
Brazen and gold.
The world has broken
Its soul,
Dark lights
Huddling in the cold.

Berry

Within the cold hood
Of winter's cloak
Berries hide
The colour
Of their withering fruit.

The chill calls
Through the snow
To a cold redness,
Sparkling
In the stiff blush
Of dark.

Small blemishes
Ablaze with red
Glow in the new snowfall,
Ruby bright,
Overblown, coy
Ecstatic
In the blown,
Succulent light.

Blown away world

Can you listen
To the world
Thrown away to the sun?
Bullrush seeds,
Scattered
And humming.
The Night is serene
In the closed cup
Of moon.
Do you listen to the world
Thrown away?
Do not grieve
For the world
Blown away.

Ceaseless is the blue blown glass
The circle of the dreaded stars,
The fires of a quiet lament
In the twilight dusk.

In every grassy blade
Grey landscapes,
Blue and myrtle,
Etch in the snowy rock of yellow
Hope's sweet scent.

so marry the stars
Until, my love,
You are sailing boats
Down the rivers of my heart,
Until the grass turns from
Brown to green
And love peeps out
Of her winter bulb.

Marry the stars my love
Until a silhouette of mauve
Remarries the light with gold,
Like sun to the swaying cornfield,
Like myrrh to the lilac flower
Remarry the stars my love.

Chastise me with your whip
I whisper your beauty.

There are few words
In this winter weather.

Be my chaperone
When the sun clouds over.

Fuse the basque,
The willow of my skin

And don't let the world
Close in.

Naked in jumbled rhyme,
Rosy and sleepy

I put on my gown
As the current of Night
Slows down,
As you uncuff me
From the eiderdown.

Do not let the geese
Catch the snowflakes
In the water,
Or let the blizzards
Fix
To the magnets of darkness.

Line the lakes with
The drift of gossamer reed,
And open wide-eyed joy,
Dipped in the wick of
Amethyst snow

Do not let the geese
Catch snowflakes
While their feathers snow,
While it is snowing.

Don't look into

The telescope of the Night
While catkins hang
Like nuggets in the sun.

Don't let the bright yarrow
Be in shadow.

Gaze at the stars,
The canaries of the dark,
And unlock
The mandolin moon,
Not the telescope
Too soon.

Gowns of youthful sounds

Birds without feather,
Grey in the grip
Of Nature's winter clutch
Stray from the branches
Of a childhood voice,

Away from Summer
And her warm jasmine
They sing in blizzards
Until the layers
Of unkept dew
Melt the forest eye
Of Winter withering,
And berries of the spotless sun.

Birds without feather
Sleep and wake,
Sleep and wake,
In sounds of youthful gowns
In gowns of youthful sounds.

I sleep in rows of *big flowers*

Scrambling in orange groves of love.
The *tall poems* listen
In and out of the flames
Of joy
Where the chambers
Of youth cloy.

In and out of
The soft burrows
Of blissfulness,
The hazelnut stories
Of *small poems*
Remember visions of violet
And I sleep in rows
Of *big flowers.*

Keepsakes

Noah makes keepsakes
In the haloes of dusk,
Makes keepsakes of the sun.

We hold hands
In the ochre sands.

You swim away
From harbours of marigold,
And the keepsakes
Twinkle like anklets
In the open wings of the sea.

And spells
Of the quiet moonlight
Dream in sea flowers
Of keepsakes holding hands,
Keepsakes holding hands.

Like sycamore seeds

The taste of the withering sun
Lingers where trees dance
In waves,
Crinkled and beautiful
In winter mufflers.

And blood-shot
As the push and pull
Of the Night traces her
She sinks
Into the blossom of dark,
Twinkling over the wake
And fall of sleep's path
Like sycamore seeds,
Hushed in the tasting
Of the broken waters of love.

Morning

Gossamer soothes the hot dry earth
Gently cradling its agitated stems
It clothes, wraps and delicately soothes
The steaming sod,
Misty, hazy white as silk dust,
Drifting lazily,
Sifting through broken leaves,
Brittle twigs and melted daisies,
Petals strewn upon the sizzling ground.

Now motionless the fragile skeletons
Of life
Nod and bob, to and fro
In the parting mist of dawn
Cocooned in a silken net of a shell,
So finely woven
That money spiders would greedily seek
To know its magic
Or even hazard to follow the secret silver steps.

Silver spins rapidly into gold
As blackbirds cast away the crumbling net
And prepare the daisies for a bath of buttermilk,
Whisk it softly until the pearls are spotted
With streaks of yellow

And the daisies can sit contentedly
In their pockets of settled speckled content.

Pecking the gold dust
Two cooing woodpigeons
Remove grit from the dusty powder of morning,
Broken breadcrumbs
Lose the daisies and their sweet content
Shove them into corners of restless uncertainty

Yet safety glides in the beaks of their hosts.
Let them peck and soothe the drifting ground
Escaping into half light shadows
Stretching out into pools of mixed ink
So the green is yellow white and gold
And buff.
Trot back to kiss the pretty heads
Of the waking daisies,
Now gone

But quiet ground remains
Resting under the tall trees
Leaning over the dusty floor.
Sweep away the dust and leave a carpet
Multicoloured and exquisite in its shading,
Now silent. Wait and be gone.

(written during a bi-polar delusion)

New lilac

The switch of lilac to gold
Unravels the silver veins
Of scowling trees
And leaves her marooned
Until golden light returns.

And a splash of silver
Is like bark to the Night,
Soft and dreadful

No nature is clinging

To the rim
Of hazy trees
And the slightest
Diminution
Jars like a knife
Between me
And your angel,
The ghost in my bed.

Does the aroma
Of December scent
Still wrap in stillness
The butterfly tails
You keep close
To the Winter sails
Of your heart?

I bid the smoke
Between the trees
Farewell
And ask every leaf
To turn her lip to me
For the baptism
Of an intimate kind.
And I let the forest flame.

Request

Give me a normal life
Nothing extreme
Nothing mundane
Just your average normal life.

Give me a normal diet
Nothing luxurious
Nothing meagre
Just your average normal food.

Give me a normal man
Nothing extraordinary
Nothing boring
Just your average run-of-the-mill man

Give me a normal self
Nothing stunning
nothing plain
Just your average run-of-the-mill woman

And that's exceptional.

Seasonal tides

Winter carries snow pigeons

Spring brings leaf bells
To green stirrings.

Summer unties blooms
From the brightest lamps
Ample and bursting.

Autumn lets love
Slip through keyholes
Of sepia light,
Forgiving the Summer
For being so bright.

How loudly the seasons fight,
beautifully lit
in brilliance
and soft colour.

The angels of the earth

Listen to the echo
Of the periwinkle
Like violet glass
Broken.

Love sleeps
Like a blanket of gold
And the corn poles
Blow like angels of the earth
In sandy circles of the sun.

Blue and yellow.

Listen to the wreaths,
Listen to the flowers of grief,
Listen to the periwinkle,
The flowing cornflower,
The angels of the earth.

The blue and yellow war

Come away to a daisy realm,

Leave the war
And the sad décor
Leave the fire,
Fizzing,
Leave the linen
Leave the kettle steaming,

Come away to a flag of snowdrops
Where land is free.
Where land is free?

The ebb

Looking back I can see
The shore hesitate,
Brushed against
The ups and downs
Of every kind of bright
Nerved wave
Ever dotted on the ocean's
Silent ebb.

Held and lost
In nature's handsome tide,
Marine petals
Float and subside,
Puzzled by the sea's open hand
And the glorious blooming sheen
She has left behind.

The hyacinth

The hyacinth is mere,
Like shades of gold-lit
Blue.
She is mere,
The water-lit
Stirring of flower-heads,
Grey shades of gold.
And she came
From a mere bulb.

The night flower

In the quiet terra
The night flower
Cracks open
The blue bell
Of the darkling Night's roaming.

She waits like
A night sailor
In a blue sea of midnight
For morning.

As if she were a scholar
In black gowns.

The petal

The iris of joy,
A blueprint of fragility
Sleeps in her mooring.

The wind blows
Just to listen
And the sun shines
Only to draw the petal
From her sling...

As she keeps on glimpsing
The Spring,
A translation of watered rain,
Whispered petals,
Coloured in the sun's bright ray
Again.

The sun quickens

And the wave
Flows like gospel oak
Between me and you.

Ebony songs
Like ghosts
Make fires
And rose dreams
Crack the bed posts
Like angels,
Lighting
The morning orange blossom.

The temptress

Beyond a rosy sunset
The temptress
Breaks figs in streams,
Snaps swirling leaves,
And leaves her boot print
In the mud.

Beyond the glossy moss
And in black
The lady
Sips tea and grows roses
In a tired old shack.

The waves cartwheel

On the milky shore
As the sun,
Layered with splashed
Magenta
Rides on the back
Of the pebbled shell
Of melancholy.

As the beaches miss
The empty slosh
Of the tide awoken
The soft silence
Of staggered spray
Is swept
Through the sprinkled
Sands.

Only solitary
For a while.

Through the archway
To the childhood land
To the blackberry
And the secrets found
In birds' wings and lilies.

Through the archway
To the unlocked gate
Of memory
Where roses bloom
To a summer song

Through the archway
To the temple of dreams
Where snowy caps on hills
Melt in the velour of Spring.

Through the archway
To fields,
I hesitate,
Through the archway
Of misty white
I see my shadow
Glistening with snow
I see the child
That I know must grow
Through the archway
I let go.

un coup d'oeil

The shapes,
green-grey dolls,
opening lips,
the robots
of the past
screeched against
my mental status.

This was not a cut,
But nerves' gash.
The shapes they were
Talking,
But not heard.

These were the days
Of shapes.
The mind cries.
These were my shapes
That disappeared.

The shapes don't fit me anymore.

What dens of peacefulness

The dens of emerald
Peacefulness
Sparkle like snow
In puddles of gold.

Rings of rain
Splutter like spells
On the pavements
Of grey.

The light green ray
Of clarity
Disappears
On the sun's crimson belt.

Bright joy,
Raining,
What dens of peacefulness
Lie in green snow,
In green grey shadow?

Printed in Great Britain
by Amazon

24389573R00020